MAXIMUM SPEED

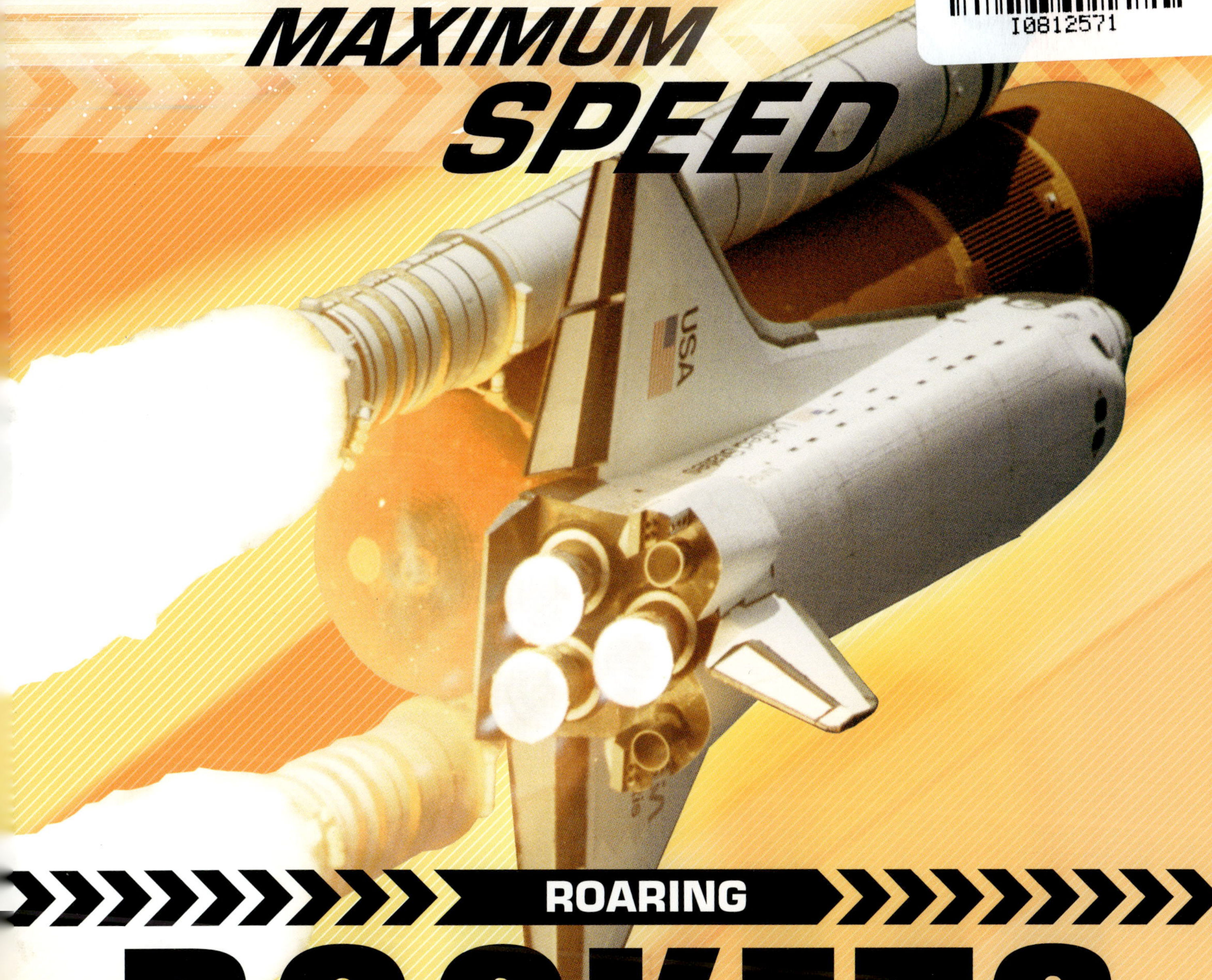

ROARING

ROCKETS

ROB COLSON

Enslow PUBLISHING

Published in 2023 by Enslow Publishing, LLC
29 East 21st Street, New York, NY 10010

Series editor: John Hort
Designer: Ben Ruocco
Produced by Tall Tree Ltd

Manufactured in the United States of America

CPSIA compliance information: Batch #CSENS23: For further information contact
Enslow Publishing LLC, New York, New York at 1-800-398-2504.

Please visit our website, www.enslowpublishing.com. For a free color catalog of all our high-quality books,
call toll free 1-800-398-2504 or fax 1-877-980-4454.

Cataloging-in-Publication Data

Names: Colson, Rob.
Title: Roaring rockets / Rob Colson.
Description: New York : Enslow Publishing, 2023. | Series: Maximum speed | Includes glossary and index.
Identifiers: ISBN 9781978531109 (pbk.) | ISBN 9781978531123 (library bound) | ISBN 9781978531116 (6pack)
| ISBN 9781978531130 (ebook)
Subjects: LCSH: Rockets (Aeronautics)--Juvenile literature.
Classification: LCC TL782.5 C66 2023 | DDC 621.43'56--dc23

Picture credits:

FC-front cover, BC-back cover, t-top, b-bottom, l-left, r-right, c-centre

FC NASA/Tony Gray/Tom Farrar, BC-Michael Taylor/SpaceX , 1 NASA, 4 guideline/Shutterstock.com, 5r Sergei Arssenev/Creative Commons, 6l NASA, 6bl LuckyVector/Shutterstock.com, 6br Meilun/Shutterstock.com, 7 US Air Force, 8t Carlos Moreno Rekondo/Creative Commons, 8b Pline, 9l US Army/NASA, 9r White Sands Missile Range/Applied Physics Laboratory, 10-11 Ebs08/Creative Commons, 11 NASA, 12tl Bill Ingalls/NASA, 12bl Asetta/Shutterstock.com, 12-13 Rodichev Vitalii/Shutterstock.com, 13t AP Photo/TASS/Mattias Malmer, 14 NASA, 15tl NASA, 15cr NASA, 16tl Ebs08/Creative Commons, 16b NASA, 16-17 NASA, 17r NASA, 18 NASA, 18-19 NASA, 19tr NASA, 19br Jack Pfaller/NASA, 20l MSFC/NASA, 20-21 Don Davis/NASA, 21b JPL Caltech/NASA, 22r NASA, 22-23 NASA, 23bl JPL-Caltech/Malin Space Science Systems/NASA, 24tr NASA, 24-25 JPL-Caltech/MSSS/NASA, 26-27 SpaceX, 26 SpaceX, 27 Space Exploration Technologies Corp., 28l NASA, 28-29 Andrzej Mirecki/Creative Commons, 30 NASA

CONTENTS

HISTORY OF

ROCKETRY

Rockets are objects that fly through the air, powered by an explosive mix of fuel. The first rockets were developed for warfare. In recent decades, huge rockets have made space exploration possible.

FIRE ARROWS

Rockets were invented in China about 1,000 years ago. They were used to fire arrows on the battlefield. Each arrow was attached to a paper tube, which was filled with **gunpowder**. As the gunpowder burned, pressure inside the tube fired the arrows through the air.

In the 15th century, Korean engineers developed rocket launchers that could fire up to 200 rocket-powered arrows at a time.

An Indian soldier uses his rocket as a flagstaff.

IRON MISSILES

In the 18th century, the army of Mysore in southern India developed a destructive new form of rocket made of cylindrical iron tubes filled with gunpowder. These were **missiles**, which are rockets that are fired at targets with the aim of causing damage. They could be fired over a range of up to 1.2 miles (2 km), and helped the Mysoreans to repel invading British troops. The British were so impressed by these weapons that they started to develop their own rockets.

MODERN MISSILES

Today, a few countries around the world have developed long-range missiles called intercontinental ballistic missiles (ICBMs). These are rockets designed to carry nuclear weapons. They have a range of more than 3,400 miles (5,500 km), traveling around Earth at heights of up to 745 miles (1,200 km). No country has yet launched an ICBM as an act of war.

The Soviet Union's R-7, made in 1957, was the world's first ICBM.

ROCKET SPEEDS

Ancient Chinese rocket
Top speed | about 124 miles (200 km) per hour
Range | up to 1,640 feet (500 m)

Mysorean rocket
Top speed | about 124 miles (200 km) per hour
Range | 0.6–1.2 miles (1–2 km)

Torpedo (U.S. Mark 48)
Top speed | 63 miles (102 km) per hour
Range | 23 miles (38 km)

ICBMs
Top speed | 17,398 miles (28,000 km) per hour
Range | 3,400 miles (5,500 km)

AIMING HIGHER

On March 16, 1926, American physics teacher Robert Goddard (1882–1945) launched a small rocket from a field in Massachusetts. In a two-second flight, the rocket reached an altitude of 40 feet (12 m) before crashing to the ground. This small experiment marked the first step in a journey that would end with sending rockets into space.

LIQUID FUEL

Goddard's small missile was the first ever liquid-fueled rocket, powered by a mix of gas and liquid oxygen. In 1920, Goddard had written a short paper called "A method for reaching extreme altitudes," in which he proposed sending a rocket to the moon. His ideas were ridiculed in *The New York Times*, which declared that rockets could not work in the **vacuum** of space. In 1969, 24 years after Goddard's death, and as Apollo 11 headed for the moon, the newspaper printed an apology to Goddard. He had been right.

EQUAL AND OPPOSITE REACTION

Goddard's liquid-fueled rockets did not need air to burn their fuel like most engines. He had correctly reasoned that such a rocket would work fine in space due to the third law of motion, as set out by English physicist Isaac Newton (1643–1723). Newton's law states that "every action has an opposite and equal reaction."

For example, if you stand on a skateboard and throw a heavy ball, you will roll in the opposite direction to the ball. In the same way, when the gases from a rocket rush out of it, this gives the rocket a push in the opposite direction, even in the vacuum of space.

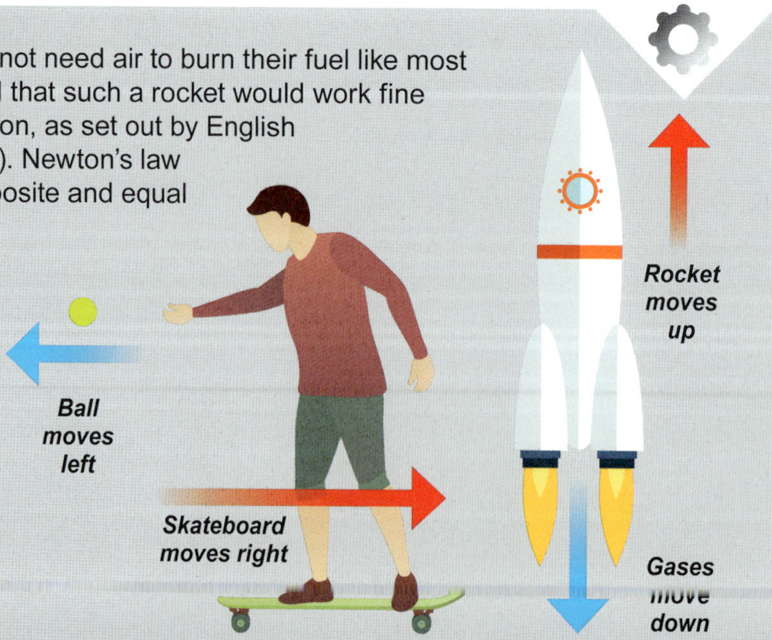

RAPID PROGRESS

Despite ridicule from the press, Goddard continued his research and by the mid-1930s, he was launching rockets to heights of more than 1.8 miles (3 km), reaching speeds of nearly 745 miles (1,200 km) per hour. Sadly, Goddard died in 1945, so did not live to see his dreams of space exploration become a reality.

THE FIRST SPACE MISSILES

Robert Goddard's work was largely ignored in his native United States. But, rocketry was taken very seriously in Germany, and the German army started a large rocket research program in 1931. In 1944, the Germans launched the first rocket into space.

TERRIFYING MISSILES

Under the leadership of aerospace engineer Wernher von Braun (1912–1977), Germany made the world's first long-range guided ballistic missile, the V2. The missiles were developed during World War II (1939–1945), and were used to bomb enemy cities, including London and Antwerp, killing thousands of people.

POWERING THE V2

Inside the rocket, the liquid alcohol fuel burned when it mixed with the liquid oxygen, creating thrust. The fuel finished burning about one minute after takeoff, at which point the engine shut off and the rocket fell toward its target unpowered.

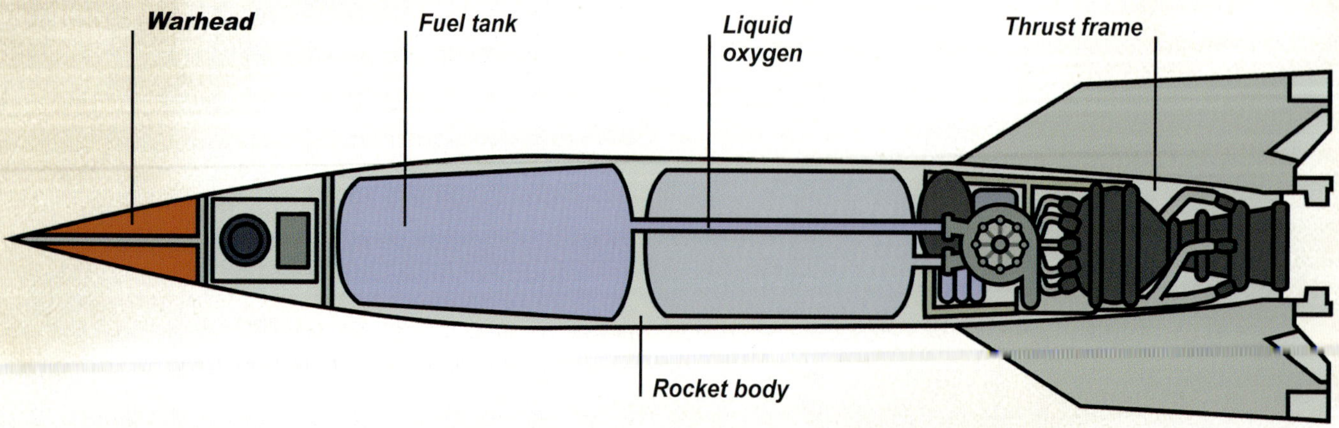

VERTICAL LAUNCH

Von Braun was mostly concerned with producing weapons, but like Goddard, he also dreamed of sending rockets into space. In a 1944 test launch, a V2 was launched vertically to see how high it could reach. It achieved a height of 109 miles (176 km), becoming the first rocket ever to fly above Earth's atmosphere.

V2 launched from Cape Canaveral, Florida.

MISSILES INTO SPACE

At the end of the war, von Braun and hundreds of other German rocket scientists were captured and secretly moved to the United States to continue their work. In 1946, the first ever photograph from space was taken from a V2 rocket launched from the United States. The age of rocket-powered space exploration had begun.

This is the first photograph ever taken from space. It was snapped from a V2 at a height of 65 miles (105 km) above the ground, just above Earth's atmosphere.

ESCAPING EARTH'S GRAVITY

The first rockets to be sent into space quickly fell back to Earth. While they had left Earth's atmosphere, they were not traveling fast enough to enter into orbit. To remain in orbit, rockets need to reach a very high speed, known as orbital velocity.

GETTING UP TO SPEED

Centuries before a rocket achieved orbital velocity, Isaac Newton imagined a cannon firing cannonballs from a high mountain. At low velocities, the cannonball falls to Earth (A), pulled by Earth's **gravity.** But if it is fired fast enough, it will enter into orbit around Earth (B). This speed is called orbital velocity. Fired even faster, the cannonball will fly off into space (C). This is called escape velocity.

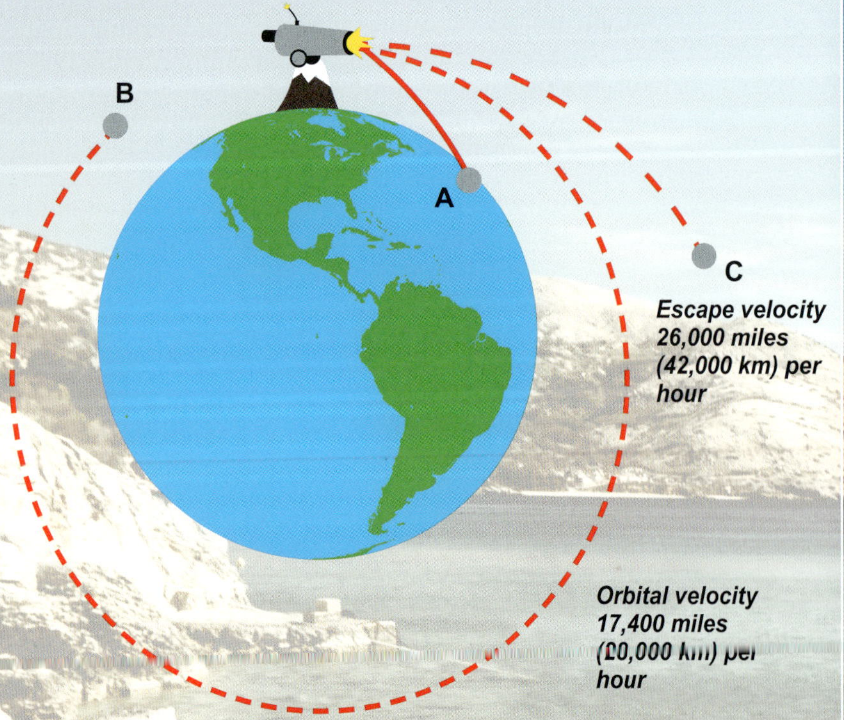

HOW A ROCKET IS LAUNCHED

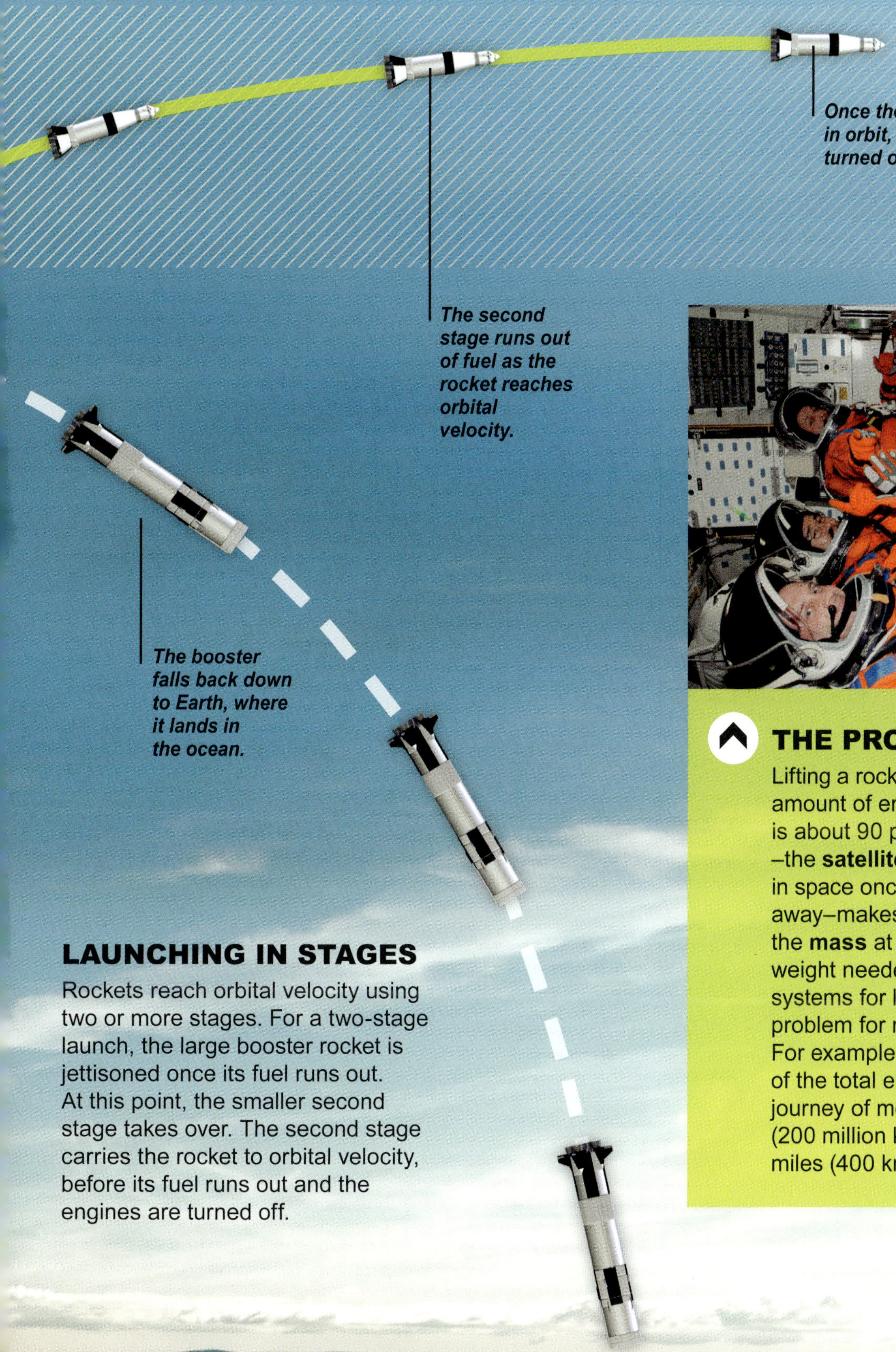

LAUNCHING IN STAGES

Rockets reach orbital velocity using two or more stages. For a two-stage launch, the large booster rocket is jettisoned once its fuel runs out. At this point, the smaller second stage takes over. The second stage carries the rocket to orbital velocity, before its fuel runs out and the engines are turned off.

THE PROBLEM OF WEIGHT

Lifting a rocket into space requires a huge amount of energy. The mass of a rocket is about 90 percent fuel. The **payload** –the **satellite** or spacecraft that will stay in space once the rockets have fallen away–makes up only about 4 percent of the **mass** at liftoff. Adding the extra weight needed for the life support systems for long journeys is a major problem for missions to distant planets. For example, on a mission to Mars, half of the total energy needed for the whole journey of more than 124 million miles (200 million km) is used in the first 248 miles (400 km) of the trip!

THE SPACE RACE BEGINS

During the 1950s and 1960s, the United States and the Soviet Union ran huge programs to develop rockets to send into space. This became known as the Space Race. The early successes in the Space Race went to the Soviet Union.

CONVERTED WEAPONS

The Soviets' early launches were made using R-7 rockets. Initially developed as ICBM weapons (see pages 4–5), the rockets were found to be far better suited to launching payloads into space. Here, one of them is seen launching a mission to the International Space Station.

INTO ORBIT

In 1957, the Soviets launched the first ever satellite, Sputnik 1. A metal sphere the size of a beach ball, the satellite remained in orbit around Earth for three months before burning up when re-entering Earth's atmosphere. It completed 1,400 orbits of Earth, traveling at a speed of 18,000 miles (29,000 km) per hour, covering a total distance of 43 million miles (70 million km).

SPACE DOG

The successful launch of Sputnik 1 was followed a few weeks later by Sputnik 2, carrying a dog called Laika. She survived for a few hours before dying from overheating. Sputnik 2 was not intended to bring Laika back, but later missions with animals were designed to be recovered.

Soviet scientists later expressed regret that they had not tried to bring Laika back to Earth alive. A monument to her has been built in Moscow, Russia.

FIRST HUMAN IN SPACE

After successfully placing more dogs in orbit and bringing them back alive, the Soviets were ready to send a man into space. The first human to enter orbit around Earth was Yuri Gagarin (1934–1968), who completed one orbit of Earth on April 12, 1961, inside the capsule *Vostok 1*. The capsule was launched into orbit by a powerful Vostok K rocket.

"Orbiting Earth in the spaceship, I saw how beautiful our planet is." Yuri Gagarin

THE CHIEF

The Soviet Union's space program was led by rocket engineer Sergei Korolev (1906–1966). Known as the "Chief Designer" or simply "Chief," Korolev's identity was kept secret to protect the program. He died in 1966 while working on a project to put the first man on the moon, a feat that would instead be achieved by the United States.

MISSION TO THE

MOON

The U.S. Apollo program put a man on the moon in 1969. This was the largest peacetime science project in history. At its peak, it employed more than 400,000 people, many of them developing the rocket technology needed for such a long journey. In total, there were 17 Apollo missions, and six of them landed on the moon. The first to do so was Apollo 11.

JOURNEY TO THE MOON

Apollo 11 blasted off on a Saturn V rocket (see pages 16–17) on July 16, 1969. It reached orbit around the moon 59 hours later, having traveled 236,121 miles (380,000 km). When Apollo 11 separated from the final stage of the rocket, it was traveling 23,612 miles (38,000 km) per hour. It slowed as it approached the moon, pulled by Earth's gravity. It had two parts: the Command and Service Module (CSM) and the Landing Module, nicknamed *Eagle*. The CSM stayed in orbit around the moon while the *Eagle* descended to its surface.

POWERING THE *EAGLE*

Seen here on the surface of the moon, the *Eagle* ascended back to the CSM powered by a rocket engine. The engine carried two kinds of liquid fuel, which were kept in separate containers. When the time came for liftoff, the two liquids were mixed together. This caused them to burn, producing upwards **thrust**. To return to Earth, the CSM had its own propulsion system, but only the Command Module section would land on Earth. The atmosphere slowed the Command Module's descent, then as it approached the ocean, three parachutes opened up to slow it further.

CLEVER SOFTWARE

Computer engineer Margaret Hamilton (born 1936) designed the **software** for the Apollo computers. She developed a system that ensured the computer would prioritize important tasks if it found itself with too much to do. When the lunar landing encountered last-minute problems, Hamilton's system made sure that it could continue. The computer on the *Eagle* could perform 40,000 calculations per second. By comparison, a modern smartphone can perform more than 2 billion calculations per second!

JOURNEY TIMES

SMART-1 (ESA)
***Journey time* | 56 weeks**
***Date* | 2003**

SMART-1 slowly spiralled outwards as it orbited Earth until it finally reached the moon's orbit. This was the slowest-ever journey to the moon, but also the most fuel-efficient.

New Horizons (NASA)
***Journey time* | 8 hours, 35 minutes**
***Date* | 2006**

In 2006, NASA's New Horizons space probe passed the moon in just 8 hours, 35 minutes. It was on its way to Pluto, and was traveling at 36,373 miles (58,536 km) per hour as it passed the moon. It would have taken a lot longer if it had needed to stop!

Luna 1 (Soviet Union)
***Journey time* | 36 hours**
***Date* | 1959**

Apollo 11 (USA)
***Journey time* | 59 hours**
***Date* | 1969**

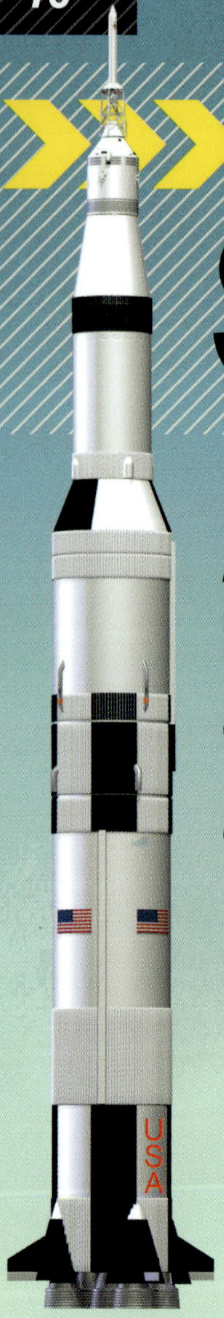

HEAVY-LIFT VEHICLE

SATURN V

The Apollo spacecraft were launched into space by huge Saturn V rockets. In their time, these were the biggest, most powerful rockets ever built. They were known as heavy-lift vehicles, and were capable of carrying payloads weighing more than 110 tons (100 mt). The rockets could only be used once, and each launch cost more than $1 billion!

Saturn V measured

364 feet

– as tall as a 36-story building.

Human to scale

THREE-STAGE LAUNCH

For a lunar-landing mission, the rockets consisted of three stages. Each stage would burn until its fuel ran out, at which point it was jettisoned and the engines of the next stage would fire up. The first two stages fell back to Earth, while the third stage remained in orbit around Earth.

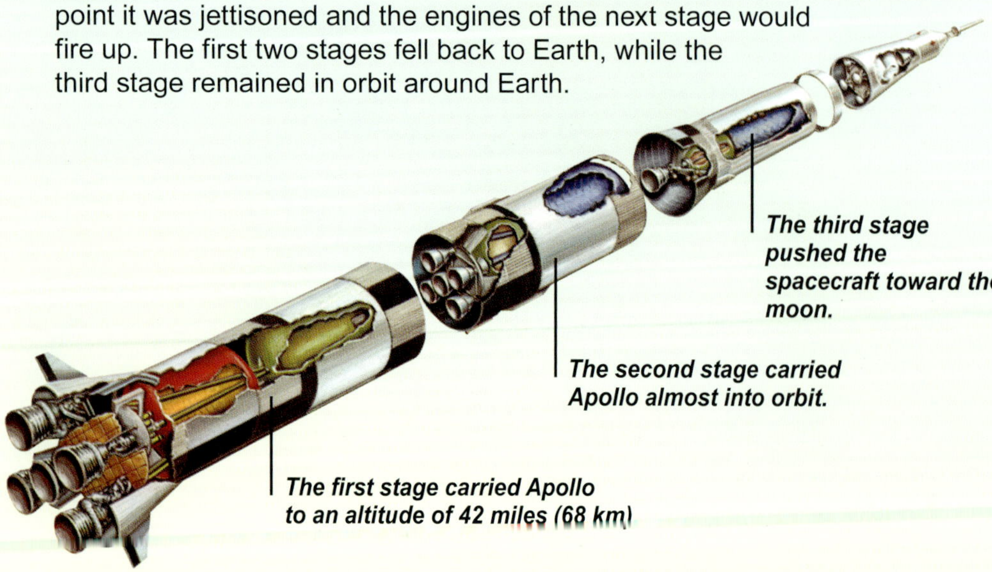

EXPLOSIVE FORCE

The first stage was the most powerful stage. It contained five rockets and burned about 20 tons (18 mt) of fuel per second. That's enough fuel to drive a car right around the world 10 times! The rockets ran out of fuel in about two minutes. The rocket generated 35 million **Newtons** of upwards thrust at launch. In its two minutes of operation, it used enough energy to power the whole of New York City for more than an hour.

Fully fueled, Saturn V weighed 6.1 million pounds (2.8 million kg)–that's more than 400 elephants.

ROCKET FACTORY

The biggest rocket in the world needed the biggest factory in the world in which to build it. The cavernous Vehicle Assembly Building (VAB) at NASA's Kennedy Space Center in Florida was constructed in 1966. Standing 525 feet (160 m) high, it is the largest single-story building in the world.

SPACE SHUTTLE

NASA's space shuttle was the first partly reusable spacecraft. It was designed to transport people and cargo to orbiting spacecraft. A fleet of five space shuttles flew 135 missions between 1981 and 2011. They were launched vertically with rockets, then flew back down to Earth like a glider.

INTO SPACE

The shuttle was carried into space attached to two rockets and a giant fuel tank. The rockets were powered by solid fuel, combining aluminium powder with a chemical called ammonium perchlorate to make an explosive mixture. Two minutes after liftoff, the fuel was all burned out and the rockets fell into the ocean, where they were recovered to be used again.

Space Shuttle Endeavour

CONTROL ROCKETS

The Shuttle was fitted with three main rockets and two orbital manoeuvring rockets on either side that it used to steer. After jettisoning the launch rockets, the Shuttle used its own rockets to place itself into the right orbit. The smaller orbital manoeuvring rockets were used to make small corrections to the orbit during the mission.

GLIDING BACK TO EARTH

The pilots needed a great deal of skill to bring the shuttle back to Earth. The shuttle first slowed itself down with its rockets, before turning the engines off and descending. At this point, it was still moving at 17,400 miles (28,000 km) per hour. Once the shuttle reached Earth's atmosphere, its wings were used to glide to the ground, making an S-shaped path to slow it down. Once it landed on the runway, parachutes opened at the back to bring the shuttle to a complete stop.

DEEP SPACE

PROBES

In 1977, NASA launched the two Voyager space probes into space, headed for the outer planets of the solar system and beyond. Today, Voyager 1 and 2 are the farthest human-made objects from Earth. They have left the solar system, but are still sending us messages as they head out toward the stars.

ESCAPING THE SUN

NASA launched the Voyager probes in 1977 in two separate launches aboard a Titan-Centaur rocket. In order to set their path out of the solar system, the probes needed to reach escape velocity from the sun, which is about 26 miles (42 km) per second, or 93,205 miles (150,000 km) per hour, at the distance of Earth's orbit from the sun. The farther from the sun they get, the slower the escape velocity. Voyager 1 is currently moving from the sun at a speed of 10.5 miles (17 km) per second.

COURSE FOR THE STARS

In 2012, Voyager 1 left the solar system and entered **interstellar space**. By 2020, it was billions of miles from Earth. That's a distance 150 times farther than the distance from Earth to the sun. It is on course for the star AC +79 3888, which lies 17.6 **light-years** from Earth. It will reach the star in 40,000 years' time. Sadly it will not be able to beam back any messages to Earth. Its power supply is due to run out in the next few years.

GRAVITY SLINGSHOTS

Spacecraft traveling through the solar system can get a boost of energy along the way from the planets. By timing their approach to a planet just right, the spacecraft receive a "slingshot" from the pull of the planet's gravity, which speeds them along their way. The Voyager probes were given gravity slingshots from both Jupiter and Saturn. This kept them above the sun's escape velocity.

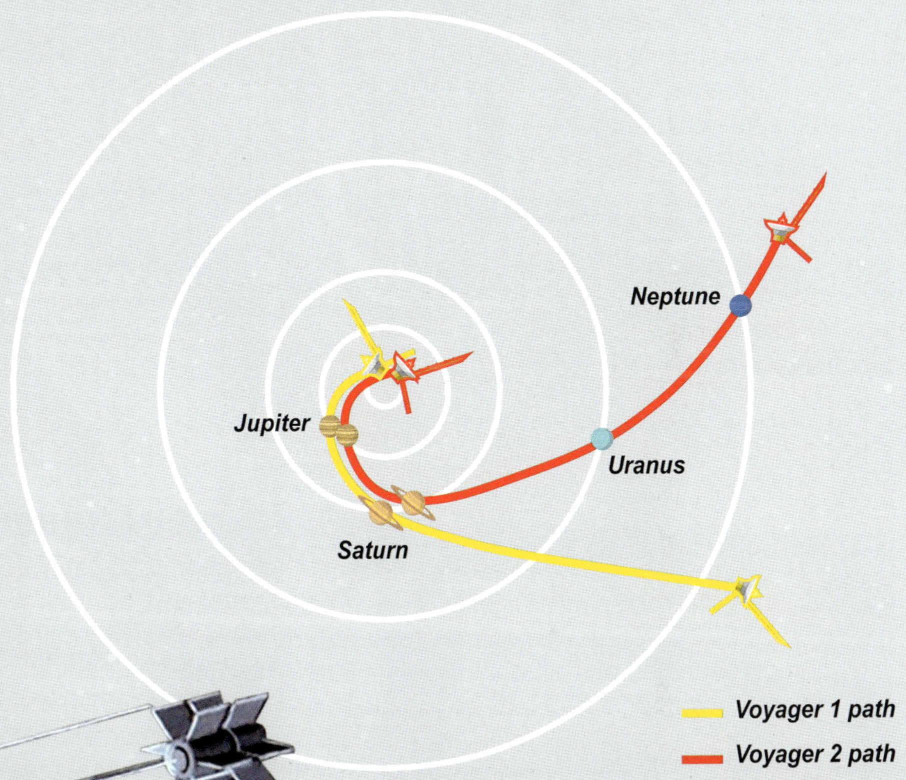

TALKING TO ALIENS

Voyagers 1 and 2 each carry a gold-plated record with recordings of sounds and images from Earth. If they ever encounter an alien life form, they may be able to tell them something about life on Earth!

FUTURE NASA

MISSIONS

The last humans to set foot on the moon were astronauts on the Apollo 17 mission in 1972. Today, NASA plans to return to the moon more than 50 years after the end of the Apollo program. The Artemis program aims to send another man and the first woman to the moon in 2024 aboard the Orion spacecraft.

SPACE LAUNCH SYSTEM

Orion will be launched into space by the most powerful rocket ever built, the Space Launch System, or SLS. It will first be tested with an uncrewed Orion spacecraft. After the first two minutes, the rocket will drop its rocket boosters, while the core stage falls away after eight minutes. The four engines burn through 740,000 gallons (2.8 million l) of liquid fuel in just eight minutes of extreme power.

LUNAR BASE

The SLS will carry equipment and supplies to the moon as well as people, and NASA plans to establish a permanent lunar base within 10 years. There, they will test out life support systems that could be used on other planets. They will also monitor the astronauts to see how their bodies cope with life on the moon. NASA hopes to use what they learn as the basis for the first mission to Mars.

COULD HUMANS LIVE ON MARS?

Sending humans to Mars presents huge challenges. Mars' gravity is only three-eighths that cf Earth, and this change affects the body in many different ways–wasting bones and muscles in a way that could be dangerous when they return to Earth. In a medical emergency, they won't be able to come home for treatment, so the astronauts will need to be totally self-sufficiert. They will need to take everything they need with them, and that will require a powerful rocket that can carry a heavy payload (see pages 26–27).

MISSIONS TO MARS

Since 1971, six unmanned missions have been sent to Mars. The most recent missions placed rovers on the surface of the planet to explore it.

ROVERS ON MARS

Four rovers were sent to Mars between 1997 and 2011. One, Curiosity, is still exploring the planet's surface, sending back photos and taking samples of rocks. This car-sized vehicle was carried into space in 2011 by the huge Atlas V rocket. The rocket was made of two stages. The first stage was powered by a mix of kerosene (a kind of oil) and liquid oxygen, while the second stage was powered by liquid hydrogen and liquid oxygen.

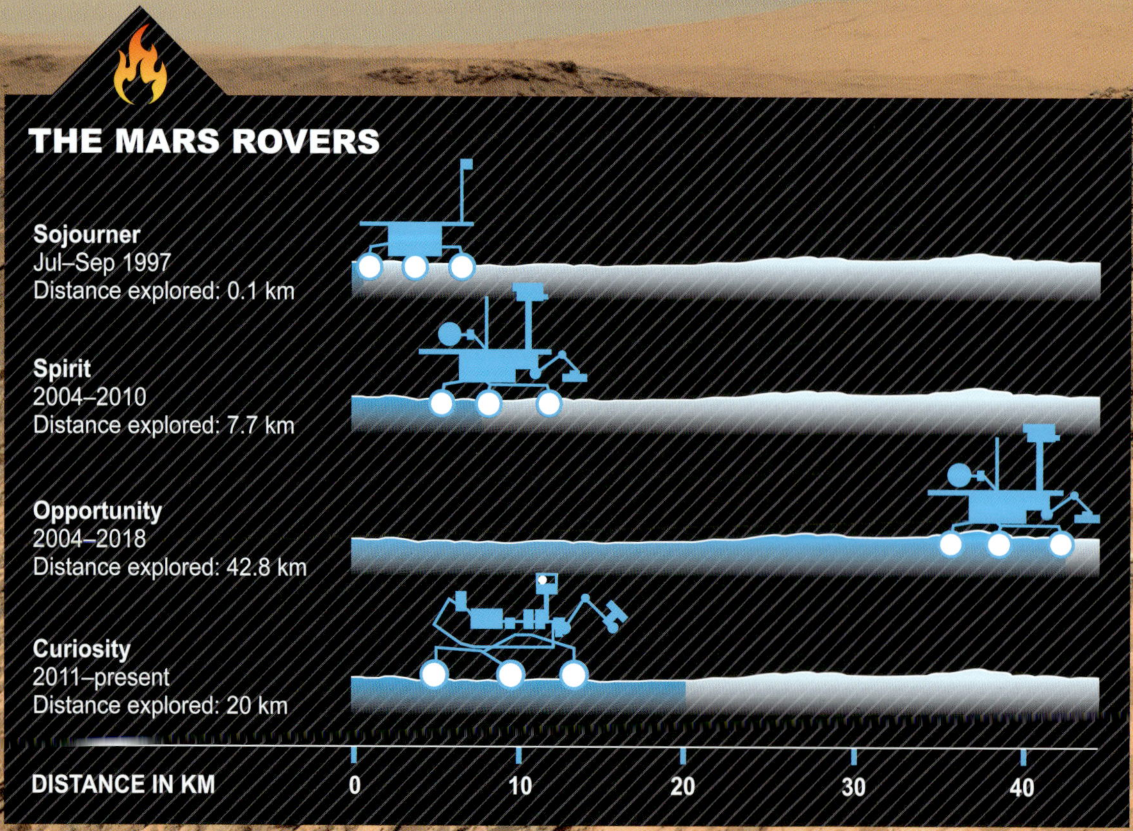

WHEN TO LAUNCH?

Scientists planning missions to Mars must choose their launch date carefully for a time when Mars is close to Earth. As the two planets orbit the sun, the distance between them varies from 34 million miles (55 million km) to 249 million miles (401 million km). Rockets are launched about three months before the closest point, when Mars is just ahead of Earth in its orbit.

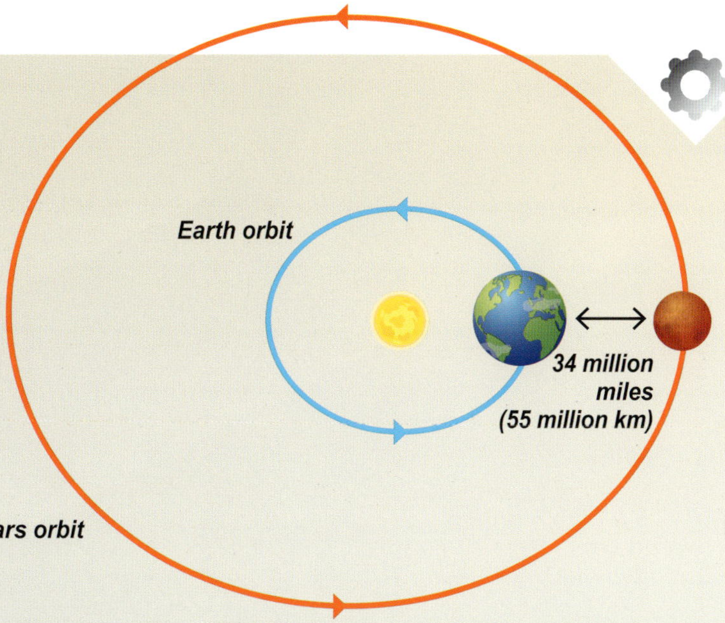

SLOW AND STEADY

Curiosity moves around Mars slowly and carefully to make sure it does not get stuck. It has a maximum speed of just 459 feet (140 m) per hour. The rover is powered by electricity produced by a store of radioactive fuel. It communicates with Earth via radio, sending back pictures such as this.

PRIVATE MISSION

SPACEX

Until recently, only wealthy countries like the United States or Russia (previously the Soviet Union) could afford to send rockets into space. Today, China and India are launching space missions, while private company SpaceX is developing a rocket to compete with NASA to send the first humans to Mars.

GIANT ROCKET

SpaceX founder Elon Musk calls his rocket design the Interplanetary Transport System (ITS). When it is built, it will be the biggest rocket ever made, standing 400 feet (122 m) high and weighing about 11,500 tons (10,500 mt)–that's three times heavier than Saturn V. It will carry a payload weighing about 600 tons (550 mt), four times the weight of Saturn V's payload.

The rocket contains a cluster of 42 engines powered by liquid fuel.

Comparison of heights between ITS, Saturn V, and a person.

FUEL FROM MARS

One of the biggest challenges for a manned mission to Mars is carrying enough fuel to complete the whole journey and to power life on Mars. SpaceX hopes to overcome this problem by making fuel on Mars itself. The first unmanned missions will establish whether the resources needed are found there. They plan to use carbon dioxide in the atmosphere and ice on the surface to make the fuel.

REUSABLE ROCKET

In addition to its ambitious plans for Mars missions, SpaceX is developing the world's first fully reusable space rocket. They hope this will slash the cost of space flight. In 2017, SpaceX's Falcon 9 rocket placed a satellite in orbit using a first stage that had previously been used the year before. The stage successfully returned to Earth for a second time, landing on a drone ship that was waiting for it in the Atlantic Ocean.

STARSHIP

Once the first rockets have detached, the SpaceX rocket that will continue to Mars is called the Starship. Once launched, the Starship will be refueled in orbit before setting off on its long journey. Before sending any humans to the planet, at least two unmanned flights will be sent with the provisions needed to build a settlement on the surface of Mars, such as electricity generators and life-support systems.

ROCKETS TO THE STARS

Robert Goddard was once ridiculed for thinking we could send a rocket to the moon. Today, many people think sending a rocket to the stars is equally unlikely. The distances involved are truly enormous, and there is a maximum speed for any craft attempting to cover it (light speed). Various solutions have been proposed.

HUGE DISTANCES

Nothing in the universe can travel faster than light, which moves at 186,411 miles (300,000 km) per second. Astronomical distances are measured using light-years, which is the distance light travels in one year–5.9 trillion miles (9.5 trillion km). The nearest star, Proxima Centauri, is 4.2 light-years away. Voyager 1 (see pages 20–21), which has been traveling through space for more than 40 years, is still less than one light day from Earth!

REACHING HIGHER SPEEDS

Over the years, scientists have proposed many different ideas to reach the speeds needed for interstellar travel. All the proposals involve enormous amounts of energy. They have ranged from exploding nuclear bombs to provide propulsion to building massive sails that are pushed along by laser beams (right). It has even been suggested that it might be possible to shrink space itself to make the distance shorter!

The fastest spacecraft ever launched was NASA's Helios 2, which was placed in orbit around the sun in 1976 at a speed of 155,340 miles (250,000 km) per hour. At that speed, it would take a spacecraft 19,000 years to reach Proxima Centauri. We will need something that moves much faster than that!

A solar sail would be pushed along by a laser beam. It could potentially accelerate to half the speed of light and reach Proxima Centauri in 12 years. However, it would need to be nearly 200 miles (320 km) in diameter, and the laser pushing it along would need nearly all the power currently produced by the entire world!

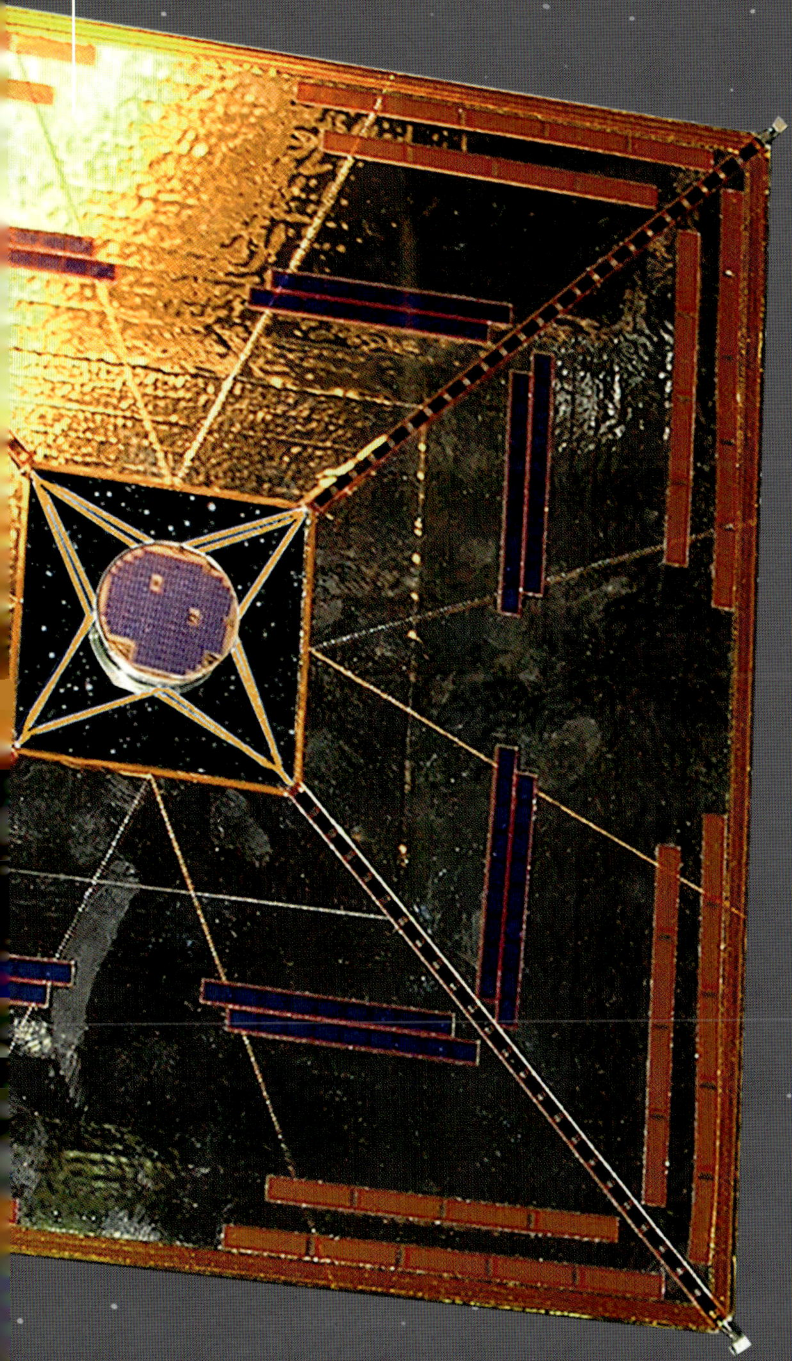

SPEED UP, SLOW DOWN

If a rocket can be developed to produce a steady amount of thrust for a long time, a journey to the stars could involve a period of constant acceleration followed by a constant deceleration. The rocket would accelerate for the first half of the journey, reaching close to light speed, then turn around and decelerate for the second half.

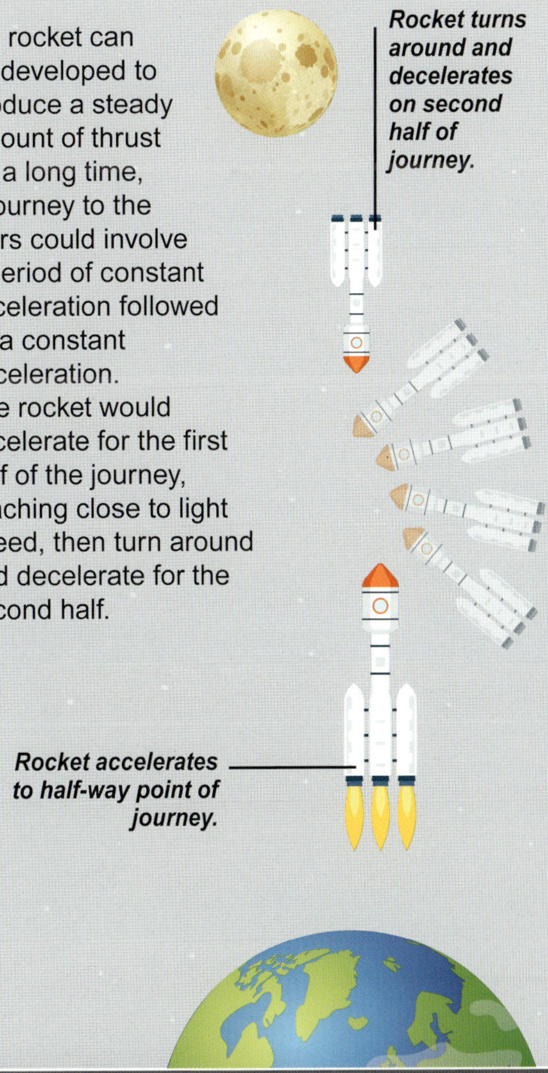

GLOSSARY

gravity
A force of attraction between objects with mass. Gravity is the force that holds us to the surface of Earth and keeps the planets in orbit around the sun.

gunpowder
An explosive substance made from a mixture of saltpeter, sulphur, and charcoal that was used to fire early guns and rockets.

interstellar space
The place beyond our solar system where the sun's magnetic field is too weak to affect its surroundings.

jettison
To throw or cast off an object.

light-year
The distance light travels in one year. Large distances in space are measured in light-years.

mass
The amount of matter contained in an object.

missile
An object that is fired at a target using a rocket or other form of propulsion.

Newton
A unit of measurement for force.

orbit
The curved path of a spacecraft or moon around a larger object such as a planet or a star.

payload
The cargo carried by a spacecraft into space.

satellite
An object in orbit around a planet.

software
A set of instructions for a computer, such as a computer program.

thrust
A force that pushes an object forward or upward.

vacuum
A volume of space that does not contain any matter.

velocity
A measure of the speed of an object in a particular direction.

warhead
An explosive head at the end of a missile.

SPEED FILE

ORBITING THE SUN
Helios 2
Max speed
155, 300 miles (250,000 km) per hour

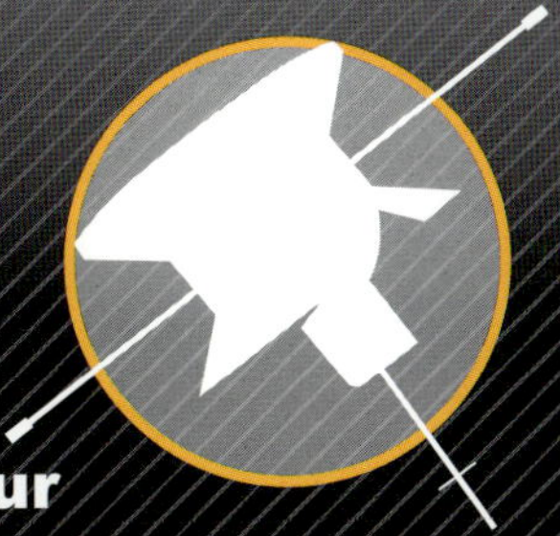

THROUGH THE ATMOSPHERE
ICBM
Max speed
17,400 miles (28,000 km) per hour

THROUGH INTERSTELLAR SPACE
Voyager 1
Max speed
37,900 miles (61,000 km) per hour

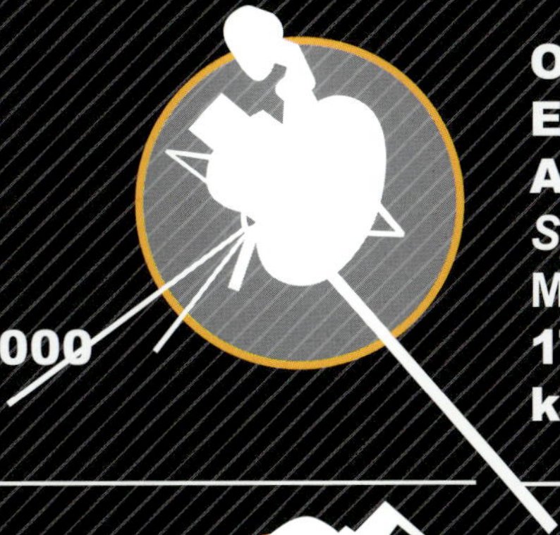

ON RE-ENTERING EARTH'S ATMOSPHERE
Space Shuttle
Max speed
17,400 miles (28,000 km) per hour

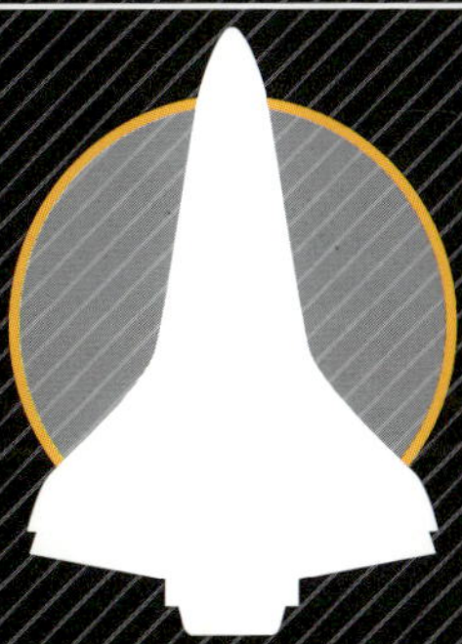

THROUGH THE SOLAR SYSTEM
New Horizons
Max speed
34,800 miles (56,000 km) per hour

ORBITING EARTH
International Space Station
Max speed
16,780 miles (27,000 km) per hour

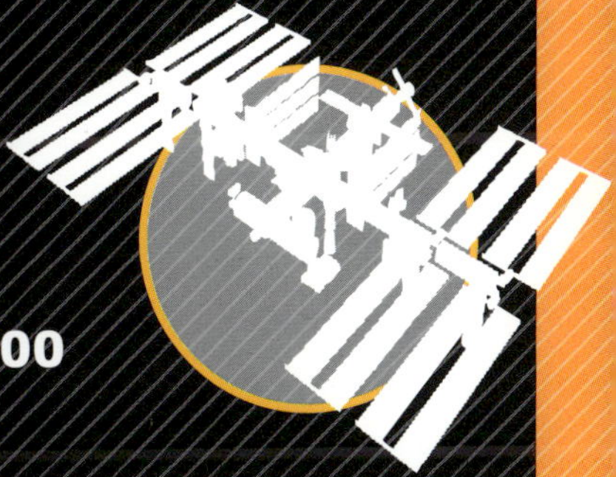

TO THE MOON
Apollo 11
Max speed
25,480 miles (41,000 km) per hour

LAUNCHED VERTICALLY
Robert Goddard's rocket
Max speed
745 miles (1,200 km) per hour

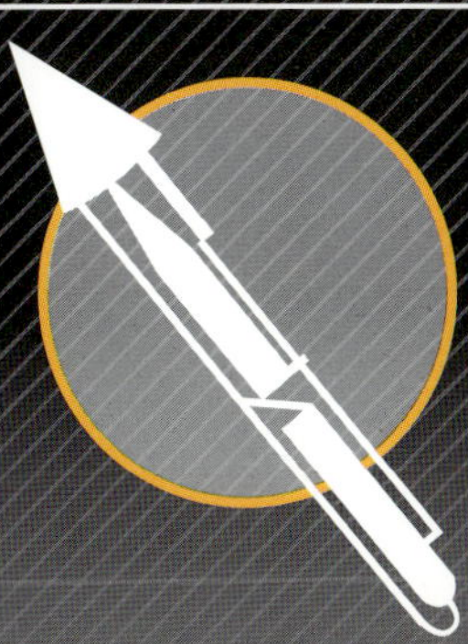

INDEX